# DEEP
# CALLS
## TO
# DEEP

## LINDA
## OTTEWELL

30 short reflections on selected Psalms

**kevin
mayhew**

# kevin
# mayhew

First published in Great Britain in 2018 by Kevin Mayhew Ltd
Buxhall, Stowmarket, Suffolk IP14 3BW
Tel: +44 (0) 1449 737978 Fax: +44 (0) 1449 737834
E-mail: info@kevinmayhew.com

## www.kevinmayhew.com

9 8 7 6 5 4 3 2 1 0

ISBN 978 1 84867 953 5
Catalogue No. 1501578

Cover design by Rob Mortonson
© Image used under licence from Shutterstock Inc.
Typeset by Angela Selfe

Printed and bound in Great Britain

# Contents

# About the author

Based in Suffolk since 1992, Linda has an academic background in modern languages and taught English as a Foreign Language before joining Kevin Mayhew Ltd in 2000 as a proofreader and editor of books and music.

Outside work, Linda is a long-standing member of her local parish church, where she plays the clarinet in the music group, is part of the prayer ministry team and regularly writes and leads intercessions in the Sunday morning services.

Afflicted with an incurable love of studying, in recent years Linda has completed theology and vocation courses by distance learning from St John's Theological College in Nottingham, and a certificate in counselling skills for pastoral care.

Music, reading and handicrafts are firm hobbies, while she can bore for England on the joys of keeping house rabbits and the benefits of Pilates as a means of exercise and relaxation!

Creative writing has been an enduring pastime and Linda is delighted to have prepared and presented her own work for publication, after many years of reading and correcting other authors' proofs.

# Introduction

Have you ever imagined yourself as a castaway on the popular radio programme *Desert Island Discs*? Along with the favourite records, book and luxury item, the guests are given a Bible as a matter of course. Now, suppose that instead of the entire Bible, you could only choose one book. Which would you go for? One of the Gospels? A favourite Letter, perhaps? Top of my list would be the Book of Psalms, the song book of the Bible: 150 rich pickings, a cornucopia of prayer, praise and worship to God. I love the Psalms!

In this collection of Psalms, many of which were penned by David, I've chosen an extract from each Psalm as a springboard for my thoughts and ideas, which are presented as a short reflection and then rounded off with a prayer or poem, a verse or two from Scripture, or part of a well-loved hymn.

It's a book to dip into when you have a few minutes. You'll find a variety of themes, including upbeat praise and worship, crying out to God for help in times of trouble, admitting doubts and fears, expressing an intense longing for God, and confessing sins.

Modern-day life may bear no resemblance to the experiences of the Psalmists, but basic human nature and emotions don't change. We can easily identify with the range of feelings expressed, as the Psalmists poured out their hearts to God in sincere, earnest prayer, holding nothing back. King David's love for his Lord and his enduring personal relationship with God shine through. He wasn't afraid to show his emotions, from the anguish and agony of spirit in Psalm 22: 'My God, my God, why have you forsaken me?' to the spontaneous exuberance of Psalm 103: 'Bless the Lord, O my soul, and all that is within me, bless his holy name.'

God has much to say to us through the Psalms and their timeless poetry gives us a language to express ourselves to God in return. We can make the words of the Psalms our own, engaging in prayer intellectually and emotionally, as we admit to God our true feelings. It's been said that the Desert Fathers regarded tears as the purest form of prayer.

We offer our whole self: heart and mind, soul and spirit, as we show our longing for a closer walk with God, who desires for us to go ever deeper with him. Our prayers should be vibrant and lead us into the very heart of God. Through these reflections, I hope to encourage you, and help you to draw nearer to God and go deeper with him.

# 1

# Staying faithful to God

They are like trees
planted by streams of water,
which yield their fruit in its season,
and their leaves do not wither.
In all that they do, they prosper.

*Psalm 1:3*

The Psalmist is describing the 'righteous', those who, by the grace of God, remain faithful to him and his ways. The Psalmist isn't saying that all who stay faithful to God will live a charmed existence, wrapped in celestial cotton wool and protected from the harsh realities of life. Like everyone else, and perhaps even more so, for we are in a constant spiritual battle, we will face problems, difficulties and failure at times. Nowhere in Scripture are we promised a life of unbroken good health, material prosperity and endless happiness.

We need to look from a different perspective and not trust this world for guidance and security. The 'streams of water' are the resources God provides to enable us to stay close to him. If we are faithful to God, walk in his ways and don't rely on sources other than him to sustain us, our 'roots' will be strong and go deep into fertile, well-watered soil. The foundations of our faith

9

will be secure and the 'fruit' we produce will be pleasing to God.

Similarly, Jeremiah 17:8 portrays an image of those who trust in God. In times of trouble, they can draw strength from him, both for themselves and for others:

> They shall be like a tree planted by water,
> sending out its roots by the stream.
> It shall not fear when heat comes,
> and its leaves shall stay green;
> in the year of drought it is not anxious,
> and it does not cease to bear fruit.

Isaiah 61:1-3, a passage quoted by Jesus in the Gospels and applied to himself in the synagogue in Nazareth, tells how God will 'bind up the broken-hearted' and 'comfort all who mourn'. Clothed in praise, instead of despair, 'They will be called oaks of righteousness, the planting of the Lord, to display his glory' (verse 3).

Spend a few minutes thinking about trees, particularly the long-established ones, as pictured in the Bible verses above. Have you ever fully considered their beauty and splendour? Such trees are often scores of years old and, like most good things, take time to grow and develop. Trees are crucial for life on our planet to continue and they can sustain countless insects, birds and other creatures. Their root system, though mainly invisible, travels deep underground to provide a firm foundation and food for the whole tree. Now focus on your 'spiritual roots'. What or who gives you stability, nourishment and vitality?

Trees are constant features of our landscape, yet deciduous trees change radically with the seasons. Autumn can be a time of breath-taking beauty for the tree, as its leaves turn colour before they are shed. Are you being called to let go of something in your life? This may seem painful but there can be no growth without change. In the depths of winter, when there is no foliage on the tree, and the skeletal branches appear to be dead, look carefully – next year's buds are already visible and, with the right resources, new life and growth in spring are guaranteed. Do you need to make any changes to bring about new growth in your life?

Lord God, thank you for your constant love and patience,
and your wonderful provision of all I need
to stay close to you and remain faithful.
I want to be strong and beautiful in your sight:
a true oak of righteousness.
Keep me close to you, I pray,
and may my roots of faith go deeper and deeper into you.
Give me courage and obedience to welcome and
embrace change and growth in my life.

# 2

# God's protection, day and night

I will both lie down and sleep in peace;
for you alone, O Lord, make me lie down in safety.

*Psalm 4:8*

David's confidence, trust and faith in his Lord shine through this verse. Even in times of fear and trouble, David is sure of God's protection, day and night. He can sleep soundly, knowing that his safety and security come from God alone and no other source: not from circumstances or from other people.

In our fraught, pressured world, stress, worry and anxiety are rife. People worry about money, their health, unemployment, loved ones, relationships, the future of our planet . . . All these, and many more besides, can be valid reasons to be concerned but some people live each day in insecurity, a dark cloud of fear and uncertainty over them. Anxiety and stress can affect concentration to the extent that total focus is fixed on the object of concern, resulting in a loss of objectivity and perspective.

The Apostle Peter writes about trusting God and putting our faith in him: 'Cast all your anxiety on him, because he cares for you' (1 Peter 5:7). At the start of Psalm 62 David says, 'My soul finds rest in God alone' (NIV). Jesus speaks gentle words of care and compassion: 'Come to me, all you that are weary and are carrying heavy burdens, and I will give you rest' (Matthew 11:28).

What are you anxious or fearful about right now? Do you take your worries to bed with you and find yourself so tense and wound up that you can't sleep easily? If you are feeling stressed, how does this affect your relationship with God? Can you trust him fully with your safety and security?

Even if you are feeling unsettled, fearful, isolated, lonely or vulnerable, you are not alone because God is with you, watching over you and protecting you, both day and night. Ask him for restful sleep. Picture yourself as a small child, snuggling down for the night in a warm, cosy bed. You can feel safe and secure, comfortable and contented, free from care and anxiety. In the stillness and quiet you are calm, with nothing to fear. This is truly a good place to rest.

Your heavenly Father longs to bless you with his inner peace, that brings release from fear and worry. His peace of heart and mind goes beyond our understanding to produce total well-being. At the end of his mission on earth, Jesus spoke words of comfort to his disciples and promised them his gift of peace: 'Peace I leave with you; my peace I give to you. I do not give to you as the world gives. Do not let your hearts be troubled, and do not let them be afraid' (John 14:27).

May our steadfast, loving God, in his never-failing care and protection, enfold you in his perfect peace.

Circle me, Lord,
keep fear and anxiety out,
keep your peace within.

# 3

# God revealed in creation

The heavens declare the glory of God;
the skies proclaim the work of his hands.
Day after day they pour forth speech;
night after night they reveal knowledge.
They have no speech, they use no words;
no sound is heard from them.
Yet their voice goes out into all the earth,
their words to the ends of the world.

*Psalm 19:1-4 (NIV)*

The richness of David's stunning poetry helps us to understand more about our Creator. The invisible God reveals himself through nature – in the majestic beauty of the sky, whether by day or night. Creation 'speaks' to us and continuously points beyond itself to show the greatness and glory of its Creator. How wonderful is our God, to have made something so marvellous as this world; to have created such a vast universe, yet to have paid attention to every intricate detail. How beautiful God must be to have imagined and created such loveliness. Creation is evidence of God's power and wisdom, and is for all the world to see.

We can't prove to anyone that God exists, but we can point them to God as revealed in his creation. The Bible doesn't set out to prove God's existence, the first words of Genesis assuming the eternal nature of our Creator God: 'In the beginning when God created the heavens and the earth . . .' (Genesis 1:1). In Genesis 1:31 we read just how pleased God was with his creation: 'God saw everything that he had made, and indeed, it was very good.' As human beings, we are the pinnacle of God's creation and stewards of his world.

Pick an aspect of creation that especially speaks to you. Finding an image might be helpful, but actually venturing outside and experiencing something of God's creation would be even better. You might want to challenge yourself by waking up early to watch the new day dawning. You may have an abiding memory of creation in all its splendour: a spectacular sunset, for instance. You could choose a beach, a landscape, a mountain, any time of day or season of the year. It's entirely up to you. As you observe creation, what does it reveal to you about God and your relationship with him? Appreciate and give thanks for what God has made and shown you about himself and his world. You may feel inspired to produce some poetry of your own!

Summer and winter, and spring-time and harvest,
sun, moon and stars in their courses above,
join with all nature in manifold witness
to thy great faithfulness, mercy and love.

*Thomas Chisholm*

# 4

# The Suffering Servant

My God, my God, why have you forsaken me?

*Psalm 22:1*

David cries out to God in his suffering, the causes of which are not clear, but involve more than physical pain. David is also suffering because of his enemies. His words were written hundreds of years before Jesus was born into our world as a baby, yet they mirror Jesus' suffering on the cross and were used by Jesus himself, as well as by the Gospel writers. Was David allowed a vision, a glimpse of the eternal truth of God's salvation plan?

At the start of the psalm David expresses how he feels rejected and abandoned by God, a sentiment echoed by Jesus in Matthew 27:46, as he took upon himself the sins of the world and suffered the anguish of being cut off from his Father, physically and spiritually, because the holy God could not look upon sin. In verses 6-8, David suffers the mental pain of being 'mocked' and 'despised' by his enemies, words similar to those used in Isaiah to describe the Suffering Servant (Isaiah 53:3) and in the Gospels, as Jesus endured mockery, humiliation and shame at the hands of the religious leaders and the crowd (Matthew 27:39-44).

Up to the end of verse 18, David provides an accurate picture of Jesus' suffering on the cross. Verses 14-17 indicate the physical agony – disjointed bones, a terrible thirst, hands and feet pierced. Verse 18 tells of his clothing being divided up by casting lots. Then the psalm becomes a song of praise and triumph (verses 22-31) for God has heard David's cry and has delivered him. Like Jesus, he was victorious.

Reflect on Christ's suffering on the cross, as he took upon himself the sins of all humanity. This was the supreme sacrifice of the innocent Suffering Servant, the Lamb of God, whose death bought our freedom and release from sin and death.

Look beyond the physical suffering to the power of the cross, the victory won, the loud cry of triumph: 'It is finished' (John 19:30). There is forgiveness and freedom at the foot of the cross.

You may like to repeat the simple words of the Jesus Prayer: 'Lord Jesus Christ, Son of God, have mercy on me.'

See from his head, his hands, his feet,
sorrow and love flow mingled down:
did e'er such love and sorrow meet,
or thorns compose so rich a crown?

Were the whole realm of nature mine,
that were an offering far too small;
love so amazing, so divine,
demands my soul, my life, my all.

*Isaac Watts*

# 5

# A special place

The Lord is my shepherd, I shall not want.
He makes me lie down in green pastures;
he leads me beside still waters;
he restores my soul.

*Psalm 23:1-3*

No psalm collection would be complete without reference to what is probably the best-known and most loved of all the psalms. The image of God as his shepherd underlines the deeply personal and intimate relationship between David and his Lord.

Like a shepherd leading his sheep to fertile pastures, where they can graze and lie in safety, the Lord takes David to a special place of security and contentment, where he can rest and relax, richly blessed by God. David is nourished and fed; his spiritual hunger is satisfied and his spiritual thirst quenched. His life and energy are restored, his soul is refreshed and revived. It's a picture of God's abundant generosity. The green pastures with soft, lush grass represent all that makes life flourish and the pure, crystal-clear waters refresh and restore well-being. This is David's 'special place' to be with his Lord and to rest in his presence, a very familiar setting from his days as a shepherd himself.

In quiet prayer, allow God to take you to a special place of blessing. You might want to use the same description as here, in Psalm 23, or your special place might recall a favourite location that you associate with rest and relaxation: the cherished memory of a past holiday, a holy place or retreat you have visited. Alternatively, your special place could be entirely imagined – a garden, a meadow, perhaps, a forest or a mountain top.

Choose a time when you don't feel pressured or hurried, and gently seek an awareness of the presence of God. Relax and unwind, letting any tension ease. Sit comfortably and still, close your eyes and be aware of your breathing becoming rhythmic and slower. Relax each part of your body, starting from the top of your head, right down to your toes. Open your hands, palms upwards, ready to receive. Simply 'be' and listen. As you build up a picture of your special place, let all your senses be involved.

Gradually increase the time you spend with God in this way, so that your special place grows and develops over the days, weeks and months. Enjoy resting in God's presence; there's no agenda, it's simply an opportunity for stillness and rest to revive and refresh you spiritually. Ignore the negative, critical voice that claims this is a waste of time, an escape from reality, or it's purely self-indulgent. We all need to be nourished and fed by God to maintain our good spiritual health and well-being, and this is one way. It isn't wrong to have 'me time', a time to be. As the old cliché goes, we are human beings, not human doings. There are seasons in life when this way of praying is needed more often and can be most beneficial. For me, personally, it proved to be my oasis of peace and comfort during a prolonged period of great unhappiness.

Jesus says: 'Come to me, all you that are weary and are carrying heavy burdens, and I will give you rest' (Matthew 11:28).

Thank you, Lord, that 'all' means me too!
I give you my burdens –
everything that's weighing me down,
holding me back
and stopping me from focusing on you.
Lead me to that special place,
where I can be with you
and rest in your awesome presence.

# 6

# Stepping out in faith

To you, O Lord, I lift up my soul.
O my God, in you I trust.

*Psalm 25:1*

Here, David is expressing his reliance on God, his faithfulness, trust and hope in him. Faith and trust are huge themes to tackle and can seem abstract concepts at times. It may be easier to look at a more concrete, visible illustration of stepping out in faith and trusting God.

One such image, from the world of nature, is that of the butterfly. Butterflies seem such tiny, insubstantial creatures with flimsy, paper-thin wings. However, they rely on air currents to lift, support and carry them as they successfully migrate across vast stretches of ocean. When a butterfly is in full flight, its beautiful colours and symmetrical wing patterns are clearly displayed, and we witness its true grace. The butterfly's ability is stretched and tested and its potential is reached. By contrast, if a butterfly's wings are closed, we only see the brown underside that provides camouflage, protection and safety.

Similarly, even though we may feel weak and frail, if we put our trust and faith in God, we are lifted by the currents of his Spirit and we truly come alive. We can experience the rich, fulfilling life that Jesus speaks of: 'I came that they may have life, and have it abundantly' (John 10:10).

We have a choice – to be timid and play it safe or to be adventurous and courageous, allowing God's Spirit to lift us and let our faith take flight. If we choose the latter, our full spiritual beauty will be seen and we can become the people God wants us to be. He knows us through and through and sees our potential, all that we can be in him. So, we can stay safe or we can step out and experience that fullness of life. As it's been said, faith is spelled R-I-S-K.

My butterfly image is only one analogy of faith and trust. How about letting your imagination run riot and expressing your ideas visually? You could doodle, draw a picture, do some clay modelling, work with textiles, stones or shells. The scope is endless and no one else needs to see your finished result, unless you want them to. See where your creativity takes you and what it teaches you about faith and trust in God. You may be surprised or even astonished! Use your visual expression as a reminder of your desire to step out in faith with God and walk with him, wherever he may lead you.

Dear Lord,
life can be difficult to negotiate
and I'm often tempted to play it safe,
choosing the easy option and sitting on the fence.

Take my weakness and frailty, my worries and anxieties
and fill me to overflowing with your Holy Spirit.
Strengthen my resolve to follow you, I pray.
I want to experience more of this abundant life with you,
life in all its fullness, as it's meant to be.
I don't want to live a half-life, hiding away in fear,
I want to be free and truly alive.
Help me to be willing to step out
and count the cost of a life lived in faith and trust in you.

# 7

# Jesus, the Light of the world

The Lord is my light and my salvation;
whom shall I fear?
The Lord is the stronghold of my life;
of whom shall I be afraid?

*Psalm 27:1*

David recognises his reliance on God and is confident that his Lord will be able to sustain him throughout his life. God is the light to guide him and his deliverer, the one he can take refuge in.

Have you ever experienced a sudden power cut at night in winter? One minute you're cosy, relaxed and watching TV, the next you're plunged into a total darkness that leaves you feeling disorientated and confused. You're grateful for the torch on your mobile phone and relieved you stocked up on candles. Even a pin-prick of light is enough to dispel the darkness.

In John's Gospel, Jesus proclaims himself to be our light, our guide through life, shining in the darkness, lighting up the way ahead, giving us purpose and direction: 'I am the light of the world. Whoever follows me will never walk in darkness but will have the light of life' (John 8:12). Through Christ, God can bring light into the darkest situations. With Jesus, there is life in all its fullness, as it was meant to be: 'I came that they may have life, and have it abundantly' (John 10:10).

Accepting the call to follow Jesus as Saviour and Lord is a conscious decision, our desire to begin a life-long journey into the heart and fullness of God's love. Along the way there is the invitation to allow more and more of God's light to shine in our hearts.

Focus on your own Christian walk and think back to the start of your journey, your initial response to God's love and all that Jesus has done for you in his death and resurrection. Is God reminding you of the first love you had for him? In the ups and downs of daily living, have you perhaps allowed something to distract you from the path of life, either deliberately, by omission or neglect? Have you begun to shut God out? Does the light of Christ need to shine more brightly in your life? Do you need to see yourself more fully through God's eyes, in his light?

If this resonates with you, it may be time for you to take stock and reassess a few priorities, asking God to restore and renew your relationship with him, to refocus your life back on him and to lead you on. Of course, this must be our desire, our conscious decision, as David himself expressed:

'Come,' my heart says, 'seek his face!'
Your face, Lord, do I seek.' (Psalm 27:8)

I heard the voice of Jesus say,
'I am this dark world's light;

look unto me, thy morn shall rise,
and all thy day be bright':
I looked to Jesus and I found
in him my star, my sun;
and in that light of life I'll walk
till travelling days are done.

*Horatius Bonar*

# 8

# Trusting God's timings

But I trust in you, O Lord;
I say, 'You are my God.'
My times are in your hands.

*Psalm 31:14, 15*


These verses speak of David's submission to God's timings and his will. In faith, David has committed his whole life into God's hands.

God is in control; he is the ruler over heaven and earth, Creator and Lord of time and space. In verse 2 of Psalm 90, the Psalmist speaks of God's timelessness and unchanging nature: 'from everlasting to everlasting you are God.' In the beginning: God; at the end of time: God.

However, this doesn't tend to stop us talking about *my* time, *my* life, as if we were in complete charge of our destiny. God has given us the ability to think for ourselves and make decisions, to plan and organise, to have hopes and dreams, aims and ambitions but we need to look to God's timings and recognise that he is ultimately in control, not us. We shouldn't behave like the people described in James 4:13-15, who disregarded God's will and went their own sweet way.

Who do you think is in control of your life? Can you honestly say to God, 'My times are in your hands' and feel peaceful about that? If you're a planner by nature (like me) who likes to be organised and in control, it can be especially difficult to submit to God's methods and timings. If something happens to disrupt my plans, and I feel out of control, I tend to panic instead of fully trusting God. I don't find it easy to admit my dependence on him (or other people), preferring to assert my own independence, trying to stay firmly in control. There was one instance a few years ago that particularly stands out, when I tried to force a situation and make something happen, even though, in hindsight, it clearly wasn't the best way forward. God gave me a picture at that time of an old-fashioned horse and carriage and there was I in the driver's seat, having snatched the reins but unable to steer a steady, successful course.

Our trust in God's timings is part of our overall submission to him, the commitment of our whole self, which is a life-long learning process. Perfect submission to the will of God brings perfect freedom to live and move within the love of Christ. However much I stubbornly try to live my life my way, I know I can't really have control of my destiny. We don't know what lies ahead, but by staying close to God, who is able to see every detail of our future, whose purposes are loving and who promises to provide everything that we need to face that future, we can go forward with a new sense of freedom.

Do you believe that God has everything in hand? In the pressures and demands of everyday life, are you patient enough to wait for God's timings? What if you discern God's voice and don't like what you hear? Where do you think what you want and what God wants for your life differ? Can you be content with whatever God has in store for you? Can you trust him?

Take my life, and let it be
consecrated, Lord, to thee;
take my moments and my days,
let them flow in ceaseless praise.

*Frances Ridley Havergal*

# 9

# God's guidance

I will instruct you and teach you
the way you should go;
I will counsel you with my eye upon you.
Do not be like a horse or a mule,
without understanding,
whose temper must be curbed with bit and bridle,
else it will not stay near you.

*Psalm 32:8, 9*

In these verses, David shows how God will guide, teach and advise us during the course of our life, but we need to pay attention to what he's saying and remain obedient to his will, and not only when his way suits us. It may take a lifetime to learn such obedience, to accept that God's way is the best and is tailor-made for each one of us. We are given choices, the free will to accept God's way or to reject it. His plan for our life isn't so rigid that it's a strict blueprint that must be followed to the last letter. There is often tension between what I believe is best for me, and being willing to follow God's path and accept his guidance.

How do you choose which way to follow? Who or what guides you and gives you a sense of direction? Jesus said, 'I am the way, and the truth, and the life' (John 14:6).

The more time we spend in God's presence, the more we will learn to recognise his voice and understand his guidance and teaching. Being obedient to God's guidance leads to peace of mind and heart. Jeremiah 6:16 speaks about choosing the right way, God's way. In the event, the people rejected God's path and followed their own instincts instead:

> Thus says the Lord:
> Stand at the crossroads, and look,
> and ask for the ancient paths,
> where the good way lies; and walk in it,
> and find rest for your souls.

Imagine a crossroads, or alternatively you might like to quickly draw one. There are several pointers indicating different directions to choose. Are you perhaps at a crossroads in your life, wondering where you will go from here? What choices are you facing? How will you seek God's help? Will you have to leave anything behind at this crossroads in order to move on?

Make me to know your ways, O Lord;
teach me your paths.
Lead me in your truth, and teach me,
for you are the God of my salvation;
for you I wait all day long.

*Psalm 25:4, 5*

# 10

# Taste and see

O taste and see that the Lord is good.

*Psalm 34:8*

Here are words of encouragement and invitation from David to make a trial, to realise that God is good. The Psalmist is sure of God's goodness because he has 'tasted' it for himself. There are some things that can only be understood by being experienced and even then, it's hard to explain them in words. We can know about God from other people or from our own reading and research but unless and until we experience him for ourselves, we will never understand his goodness.

We need to take that step of faith and accept God's invitation to come to his banquet of blessings, where his riches and gifts are presented to us, there for the taking, by his grace. Once experienced, we are invited to go deeper and discover more of God's goodness, mercy and abundant blessings, to know the fullness and all-sufficiency of God in Christ. We marvel that the infinite, almighty God, holy and majestic, can be known by us and is as near to us as a parent to a child, in an unbreakable bond of love, care and intimacy. As Jesus taught us, God our Father is our *Abba*, our 'Daddy'.

What's your favourite food, one that you would never grow tired of ordering in a restaurant? Think about why you love it so much; you may even have some to hand to remind you. Now imagine that a friend is describing to you their favourite food, one that you've never tried before. You listen to them explaining why it's so good and because of their enthusiasm and encouragement, you try it and find that you love it too. Unless you'd tasted the food for yourself, you would never have known. As Christians, we have a responsibility to tell others about our faith and its importance to us. People who are genuinely seeking God for themselves won't try to trip us up with arguments about complicated faith issues. They will want to hear about our own experiences of God and, with our encouragement, may begin to taste for themselves his goodness and mercy.

My prayer is that you will experience more and more of God's goodness in your life. May Christ, who has made his home in your heart, keep you strong and may your roots of faith go deeper and deeper into God's love. As Paul prayed for the Christians in the Church at Ephesus:

I pray that, according to the riches of his glory, he may grant that you may be strengthened in your inner being with power through his Spirit, and that Christ may dwell in your hearts through faith, as you are being rooted and grounded in love. I pray that you may have the power to comprehend, with all the saints, what is the breadth and length and height and depth, and to know the love of Christ that surpasses knowledge, so that you may be filled with all the fullness of God.

*Ephesians 3:16-19*

# 11

# The fountain of life

For with you is the fountain of life.

*Psalm 36:9*

David describes a source of pure, sparkling water, cool and totally thirst-quenching. God has given us his Son, Jesus, the water of life that can satisfy all spiritual thirst. When Jesus spoke to the Samaritan woman at the well, he told her: 'Those who drink of the water that I will give them will never be thirsty. The water that I will give will become in them a spring of water gushing up to eternal life' (John 4:14).

Just as the body needs food and water to sustain it and make it strong, so God provides all we need for our spiritual nourishment. Yet the Old Testament records many occasions when God's people preferred to go their own way and came unstuck. The prophet Jeremiah sums up their failure to remain faithful to God:

> For my people have committed two evils:
> they have forsaken me,
> the fountain of living water,
> and dug out cisterns for themselves,
> cracked cisterns that can hold no water.

*Jeremiah 2:13*

God offered his people abundant life, every resource they needed to sustain them and instead they chose the spiritual equivalent of trying to collect rainwater in their own broken vessels.

Can you recall a time in your life when you were extremely hot and parched? Do you remember how you quenched that overriding thirst and how good it felt to find refreshment and relief? Now look at your spiritual life and the resources you depend on for your journey of faith. How willing are you to receive the 'spring of living water' to refresh and sustain you? What do you put your trust in? Be honest – money, your job, yourself, other people . . . The world presents many attractions that will eventually fade and fail, including money, power and security. How often do you behave like the people Jeremiah wrote about, trusting in other resources, ultimately 'idols', to nourish you? In Revelation 21:6 the Lord gives us this wonderful promise of spiritual refreshment, offered without cost: 'To the thirsty I will give water as a gift from the spring of the water of life.'

I heard the voice of Jesus say,
'Behold I freely give
the living water; thirsty one,
stoop down and drink and live.'
I came to Jesus, and I drank
of that life-giving stream;
my thirst was quenched, my soul revived,
and now I live in him.

*Horatius Bonar*

# 12

# Open to God

Be still before the Lord,
and wait patiently for him.

*Psalm 37:7*

One day last year in early summer, it was warm enough to sit outside and read. The garden was sunny and I was surrounded by bright flowers. After some time, a peacock butterfly landed on the open page of my novel and began to preen itself. I watched, fascinated by each detail of its tiny body and kept completely still.

Once the butterfly had finished this cleaning regime, it spread out its wings, soaking up the sunshine. Then the creature's full beauty was revealed and I was captivated by the intricate design, colour and symmetry. The butterfly and I remained still for some time, until, disturbed somehow, it suddenly flew off, leaving me quite sure that this had been a special time to cherish and remember.

God speaks to us in different, sometimes unexpected ways and on that day, it was in a 'chance' encounter with a butterfly. In our impatience, we may ask God to speak to us, yet don't wait quietly for him to do so, or we expect him only to respond in certain, familiar ways. It's easier to try and dictate to God, rather than sit and wait quietly, open and responsive to him. Unless we are patient, we may overlook how God chooses to speak and so miss the moment.

God's word tells us that he is always with us, even if most of the time we are caught up in the busyness of life and overlook his presence. Ask yourself when you last took time to be still in the presence of God and gave him your full attention. However busy you find yourself, set aside a few moments during the course of the day to sit with God and wait quietly for him to speak. You may be surprised or even astonished at the outcome!

Lord, forgive me for the times I dictate to you.
It's truly ridiculous that I should try to tell you
when and how to speak.
Close my mouth for a while
and let me be ready to receive from you.
Help me to be more patient
and to wait in the silence,
without rushing away.

# 13

# God's presence in times of trouble

I waited patiently for the Lord;
he inclined to me and heard my cry.
He drew me up from the desolate pit,
out of the miry bog,
and set my feet upon a rock,
making my steps secure.
He put a new song in my mouth,
a song of praise to our God.

*Psalm 40:1-3*

David prays to God for release from his present situation. What his difficulty was isn't made clear, but it could have been depression or disease. David feels helpless, unable to climb out of his 'miry pit' by himself. There is no quick fix but eventually, after a period of waiting, God delivers David from his despair and blesses him, David's response being heartfelt praise to God in song.

Many people in our society today can identify with David's 'desolate pit' and 'miry bog'. We hear that loneliness and isolation, fear and anxiety are all on the increase. Many are affected by depression, or overcome by panic attacks, unable to function as they once did. When energy is sapped and motivation drained, drive and purpose lacking, the smallest thing becomes too much effort, leaving the sufferer feeling hollow and empty inside, swamped and floundering. Depression may lead to an inability to sleep and a lack of appetite, or even to feelings of hopelessness and despair, life seeming pointless. Medical help seems to offer little visible improvement in the short-term and the longed-for breakthrough fails to come.

If the 'miry pit' image describes where you are right now, a dark, desolate place and the negative feelings trip off your tongue: downcast, disillusioned, depressed, despairing, defeated . . . you may feel too exhausted to do anything, least of all pray. You may be thinking that David's example is all well and good, but your faith and trust aren't so strong and in any case, didn't David have a special relationship with God? Patience and hope ran out some time ago. You cry out to God but it's as if he doesn't care or isn't listening. Maybe he isn't even there.

Others are lifting you up in prayer, yet God still seems deaf to your predicament. 'Prayer changes everything' may be true but it's a meaningless platitude right now and all you feel is anger and frustration. You cry out: 'Where is God in all of this? Why doesn't he do something to help me?' You have forgotten the times in the past when God rescued you, or any faint memory doesn't seem relevant to what you're going through now.

Finally, exhausted from crying and tears all shed, in the darkness you discern a soft, rhythmic breathing, scarcely audible. Somehow you sense that this is the

Breath of God, God's presence by your side in the desolate place. Has he been there all the time? Then you begin to make out a shadowy figure sitting alongside you, casting the faintest of lights. A gentle, reassuring whisper reaches you: 'Remember, I am with you always', and your Saviour enfolds you in his love.

My precious child, I have loved you with an everlasting love.

# 14

# Going deeper

Deep calls to deep in the roar of your waterfalls;
all your waves and breakers have swept over me.

*Psalm 42:7 (NIV)*

Psalm 42 describes a time of great anguish, despair and spiritual depression in the writer's life. He longs to be with God at the Temple in Jerusalem, which he's prevented from doing because of his present circumstances. Even though the Psalmist knows that God is not only to be found in the Temple, he feels far from God, forgotten by him. He remembers the special communion with God during the great festivals in Jerusalem. He needs God's comfort and healing, and a release from the mocking and taunts of his enemies, a second reason for his depression. Despite his discouragement, the Psalmist won't give in or rest till his relationship with God is restored. He focuses on God's goodness, and puts his trust and hope in God to help him. Soon he will praise God once more.

To go deeper with God, we must hunger and thirst for him in the same way the deer pants for water to relieve its overwhelming thirst, as the opening two verses of the psalm describe. The water also represents safety – the deer can run into the water and the predator can no longer detect its scent. Verse 7 pictures the great distress of the Psalmist, comparing it to raging waterfalls and thundering waves crashing over him. This image can also be understood to be the powerful call of God from heaven, the force of God's love from the depths of his heart. The waves roll over the dry places and stir something deep in our heart, a longing and willingness to go deeper with God. It is the Spirit of God touching our hearts and minds. Going deeper with God can be scary and risky. We live in a world where there are countless distractions, where it's easy to avoid the hard questions and swim in the shallows instead.

Do you hunger and thirst after God, desiring to go ever deeper, or are you content with coasting along? What's holding you back? Do you try to steer a steady course, protecting yourself from risk, keeping to familiar paths? Are you willing to step out in faith and be at peace upon the open sea? To be adventurous and not always play it safe? To cast your net wider and deeper, as Jesus told his disciples (Luke 5:4-7)?

O Love that wilt not let me go,
I rest my weary soul in thee;
I give thee back the life I owe,
that in thine ocean depths its flow
may richer, fuller be.

*George Matheson*

# 15

# STOP!

'Be still, and know that I am God!
I am exalted among the nations,
I am exalted in the earth.'

*Psalm 46:10*

You know how it is: you're worn out, run ragged, pulled in all directions and everyone wants a piece of you. Juggling frantically to keep all the plates up in the air at the same time, you somehow keep going beyond the point of exhaustion, even though it'll all catch up with you sometime soon and you'll collapse in a heap. It's madness but you keep going.

You haven't intentionally stopped reading your Bible regularly and surely God knows how busy you are at the moment? After all, you've been working hard for God all this time, so praying on the move is ok, isn't it? Except it's hard to concentrate for more than a couple of minutes and the distractions come thick and fast. Before you know it, and however unintentionally, God has been side-lined and his voice drowned out by the clamour of daily life. There's been no time to spend quietly with God in his presence, seeking his will.

Finally, God has to shout to be heard, and it's not the gentle whisper that Elijah experienced, but loud thunder that booms over the busyness. Unmistakeably, it's God who is speaking and he won't be ignored: 'That's enough! Stop what you're doing, right now and listen to me!' It's time to refocus, put things in perspective and ask yourself what's *really* important in your life. Where does it get you, all this chasing your own tail? Could it be that your energy is being expended needlessly? If only you'd asked for God's help and guidance much earlier, instead of trying to go it alone.

There's no need to start feeling too guilty, though. God understands how and why this has happened to you. Instead of chastising you, he's offering a solution, a lifeline, reminding you that he is with you (Psalm 46:11) and giving you the opportunity to find a resting-place in him, amidst the apparent mayhem of life. Take it right now, don't delay! Don't be like the people the prophet Isaiah wrote about, who ignored God's message to them:

> In repentance and rest is your salvation,
> in quietness and trust is your strength,
> but you would have none of it.

*Isaiah 30:15 (NIV)*


I heard the voice of Jesus say,
'Come unto me and rest;
lay down, thou weary one, lay down,
thy head upon my breast.'
I came to Jesus as I was,
so weary, worn and sad;
I found in him a resting-place,
and he has made me glad.

*Horatius Bonar*

# 16

# God's mercy and forgiveness

Have mercy on me, O God,
according to your steadfast love;
according to your abundant mercy
blot out my transgressions.
Wash me thoroughly from my iniquity,
and cleanse me from my sin.

*Psalm 51:1, 2*

Nathan the prophet confronted King David and exposed his sin. David had committed adultery with Bathsheba and had her husband killed, so that David could marry Bathsheba himself and cover up his wrongdoing. In doing so, David sinned against God and against many other people. The words of this psalm express David's admission of guilt. In humble, heartfelt repentance he confesses his sin and asks God for mercy, forgiveness and cleansing.

David seeks a renewed purity, obedience and faithfulness: 'Create in me a clean heart, O God, and put a new and right spirit within me' (verse 10). He trusts God's mercy and forgiveness, believing that he has been pardoned and purified and is once again 'right' with God. God's forgiveness leads David to praise and worship: 'O Lord, open my lips, and my mouth will declare your praise' (verse 15).

Sin isn't a popular word nowadays. It describes anything that separates us from God, creating a barrier, distancing us from God, who wants us to enjoy close fellowship with him and experience his full and complete life. Because of Jesus, his sacrifice on the cross for us and his victory over sin and death, we can have the assurance of God's forgiveness and cleansing from sin.

Do you find it hard to forgive yourself? Do you find yourself confessing the same sin, again and again? Are you carrying round unnecessary burdens? Remember the words from the first letter of John: 'If we confess our sins, he who is faithful and just will forgive us our sins and cleanse us from all unrighteousness' (1 John 1:9).

If David's words reflect something of how you are feeling, use the whole psalm as a prayer to God. Admit your wrong, say sorry and ask for God's mercy and forgiveness. Trust in his cleansing and respond with thanksgiving and praise. Restored, you can walk in newness of life with God.

If you, Lord, kept a record of sins,
Lord, who could stand?
But with you there is forgiveness,
so that we can, with reverence, serve you.
*Psalm 130:3, 4 (NIV)*

For as the heavens are high above the earth,
so great is his steadfast love towards those who fear him;
as far as the east is from the west,
so far he removes our transgressions from us.
*Psalm 103:11, 12*

# 17

# Longing for God

O God, you are my God, I seek you,
my soul thirsts for you;
my flesh faints for you,
as in a dry and weary land
where there is no water.

*Psalm 63:1*

King David, under great pressure because of his son Absalom's rebellion against him, had to flee for his life from Jerusalem into the wilderness of Judea. Alone with God in the hardship of the desert, David pours out his heart, in a passionate and intense longing for God's presence, provision and protection. David's whole being cries out to God in his hunger and thirst, weariness and loneliness. Even in the desert, David's priority is to seek God with all his heart and to worship him.

The psalm continues with David remembering how he praised God in the sanctuary. David's confidence is in God's steadfast love and he trusts God to protect him from his enemies. When they have been overcome and David has been delivered from his present troubles, he will be able to worship in the sanctuary once more. David feels satisfied and contented, and can praise God despite the circumstances he finds himself in.

He feels safe and secure: 'in the shadow of your wings I sing for joy' (verse 7). David shows absolute faith in God and is totally committed to following him.

What does it mean to seek God? Do you have the same desire and longing for God as David expresses? Sometimes we need solitude, time away from other people to seek God. The Bible records how Jesus took himself away to quiet places to be alone with his Father (Mark 1:35). If we truly love God, we will want to spend time with him in prayer. Is God the centre, the Lord of your life? Do you want to go deeper with him and experience more of him in your life? God is infinite – there's always more. How do you keep your passion for God alive?

Be thou my vision, O Lord of my heart;
naught be all else to me, save that thou art –
thou my best thought, by day or by night,
waking or sleeping, thy presence my light.

*From the Irish, translated by Mary Elizabeth Byrne*

# 18

# God's blessing

May God be gracious to us and bless us
and make his face to shine upon us,
that your way may be known upon earth,
your saving power among all nations.

*Psalm 67:1, 2*

In this prayer for God's blessing, the Psalmist's reasoning is that other nations will pay attention and won't fail to notice how God blesses his people, with the result that God's salvation can be known by all nations.

What exactly does it mean to seek God's blessing? If we say to someone, 'God bless you', what are we asking God to do? These verses from Psalm 67 are based on the Old Testament Aaronic Blessing, when the High Priest of Israel would use these words to bless the people:

The Lord bless you
and keep you;
the Lord make his face shine upon you
and be gracious to you;
the Lord turn his face towards you and give you peace.

*Numbers 6:24-26 (NIV)*

The blessing asks God to show his mercy, compassion and favour to the people and protect them, to give them his approval and acceptance, and the peace that brings wholeness, harmony and well-being. By asking God to bless someone, we are asking him to show them his love and care.

Use the blessings from Psalm 67 and Numbers to pray for others. This shouldn't be restricted to the people we like. Jesus commanded us to love and pray for our 'enemies' and those who 'persecute' us (Matthew 5:44), the people we find it difficult to get along with, are at odds or in conflict with. Visualise the person and try to picture God's blessing going out to them, knowing that he wants the very best for them. As you pray, ask God to show you what that person needs. It might be God's forgiveness, strength and courage, or more of his joy and peace in their life. If necessary, pray for God's help to change your attitude towards this person.

Praise God from whom all blessings flow;
praise him all creatures here below,
praise him above ye heavenly hosts;
praise Father, Son and Holy Ghost.

*Doxology, by Thomas Ken*

Pardon for sin, and a peace that endureth,
thine own dear presence to cheer and to guide;
strength for today and bright hope for tomorrow,
blessings all mine, with ten thousand beside!

*Thomas Chisholm*

# 19

# My heart's desire

Whom have I in heaven but you?
And there is nothing on earth that I desire
other than you.
My flesh and my heart may fail,
but God is the strength of my heart and
my portion for ever.

*Psalm 73:25, 26*

Earlier in this psalm (verses 2, 3), the writer took his eyes off God for a while and began to envy the prosperous and 'the wicked', whose lives appeared to be very comfortable and free of troubles. Why bother to be good and righteous, when it doesn't seem to pay? He felt bitter towards God, and was tempted to give up. Then the Psalmist looked to God (verse 17), corrected his perspective and realised that nothing is more important than God, who sustains him and provides his security.

Take a look at the brightly-lit shops on any high street or watch the adverts on TV, especially round Christmas time. Materialism is so inbuilt into our consumer society that its effects on us can be easily overlooked. Some people search for happiness and contentment in material wealth, acquiring 'stuff', hoping it will satisfy them, bring them security and fulfil their lives, which it can, to some extent.

In his Sermon on the Mount, Jesus warned against storing up treasures on earth, which may glitter with false glamour for a while but can only ever be temporary. Instead, Jesus told his followers to store up lasting treasures in heaven. Whatever we treasure the most, where our heart is, will determine how we live (Matthew 6:19-21).

De-cluttering is a familiar concept these days; getting rid of unnecessary things, living more simply, in a bid to find greater freedom from possessions. Think about whether it's time to do a spot of de-cluttering in your life, so the treasures of this world loosen their grip on you, enabling you to travel more lightly and better focus on treasure in heaven.

What are the most precious things in your life? Try putting them in order of importance. If you lost them, what then? Are there some things you could live without? How easy would you find it to let go of them? Consider the difference between what you might want and what you truly need. Where does your treasure lie? Who or what is your heart's desire?

Riches I heed not, nor man's empty praise,
thou my inheritance, now and always:
thou and thou only, first in my heart,
High King of heaven, my treasure thou art.

*From the Irish, translated by Mary Elizabeth Byrne*

# 20

# Time flies . . .

The days of our life are seventy years,
or perhaps eighty, if we are strong; . . .
they are soon gone, and we fly away . . .
So teach us to count our days
that we may gain a wise heart.

*Psalm 90:10, 12*

Without wishing to sound morbid, life is short. Yes, some parts of the world enjoy a longer lifespan than the Psalmist indicates. Nevertheless, in the light of eternity, our days on earth are brief, and realising this, we should use our time wisely. Such thoughts might send some people into overdrive, trying to squeeze every drop of usefulness from each day, in a bid to leave something lasting and valuable for posterity. In our frenetic world, the anxious cry is frequently: 'I haven't got enough time for . . .' and it's often on my lips too. Yet I still find time for the things I really want to do.

The older I become, the cliché of time racing by ever faster seems true, but time doesn't change: each twenty-four hours is the same length. Regardless of whether our clocks and watches are accurate to the last split-second, we can't *make* time, and trying to *save* time is often fruitless. How reassuring it is that there will be no need for clocks or watches in eternity and we will be set free from the restrictions and boundaries of time.

I have struggled with the subject of time and how to work out my priorities for each day. I have been guilty of too much clock-watching, treating my day like a time and motion study. In recent years, it's become easier to welcome each twenty-four hours as an entity, to give thanks to God for the new day and ask him to bless it, trusting that, with his guidance, I will spend it wisely and not waste my time. I find myself living more in the present, focusing on the here and now, which I am able to do something about, with the experience gained from the past and with an eye to the future.

Think of a clock face – you might like to draw one. The numbers are in place but there are no hands. What time is it in your life? Place the hands on the clock where you feel they best fit. How do you think your life is progressing at the moment? Is it smooth and steady, or full of problems and difficulties? Do you feel as though you are standing still, going nowhere right now? Are you content, happy, sad, lonely or fulfilled? Are you carrying regrets? Is this a time of new beginnings for you? How have you arrived at this point in time? You may find it helpful to write down your reflections. Spend some time praying through them and listen for God's response.

Lord God,
Creator and Lord of time and eternity,
timeless One, beyond time,

who sees the whole of history
in a blink of the eye.
You chose to give me life.
Even before I was born,
you planned and recorded the length of my days
and that comforts and reassures me.
You know everything about me
and you are in control of my destiny.
Teach me to listen to you,
to go at your pace each day
and live within your will for my life.
Let me rejoice and give thanks for every new day,
a present from you.

# 21

# God's protection in times of trouble

He will cover you with his feathers,
and under his wings you will find refuge.

*Psalm 91:4 (NIV)*

The Psalmist's image is of a mother hen gathering her chicks close to her in a time of danger, spreading wide her protective wing feathers and completely covering her chicks with them. Instinctively, the mother hen acts to protect her brood, shielding the chicks with her own body; offering herself, if necessary, to preserve their lives.

Our Father God is compared to the mother hen, offering us refuge and safety in times of trouble and protecting us. This theme is echoed elsewhere in the psalms:

In the shadow of your wings I will take refuge,
until the destroying storms pass by.

*Psalm 57:1*

For you have been my help,
and in the shadow of your wings I sing for joy.

*Psalm 63:7*

In the Gospels, it's recorded how Jesus spoke about Jerusalem: 'How often have I desired to gather your children together as a hen gathers her brood under her wings, and you were not willing!' (Matthew 23:37).

For the Christian, there is no promise of exemption or protection from trouble, which might be in the form of bereavement, illness, disappointment or personal tragedy. Jesus himself told his disciples: 'In this world you will have trouble' (John 16:33, NIV). The promise is that our faithful God will be with us in and through times of trouble, offering strength, support and the security of his love and care.

If you are currently facing difficulties, you may not be able to change your circumstances, but you don't have to be defined by what you are experiencing; you can change your perspective. Draw strength from God. There are times in everyone's life when we need to take refuge in the shadow of God's wings. In the storms of life, when life is most challenging, you can be safe and secure in God's love, where he offers rest for your soul, heart and spirit. Learn to dwell in his presence, regardless of the circumstances of life you are passing through. No storm can destroy you when you take refuge in God. Put your trust in him and hold on to his wonderful promise, that whatever happens to you in this life, nothing can ever separate you from God's love (Romans 8:38, 39). Even if all else fails, the unbreakable lifeline of God's love will remain, like an umbilical cord connecting you to him.

The eternal God is your refuge,
and underneath are the everlasting arms.

*Deuteronomy 33:27 (NIV)*

In the shadow of your wings
my soul has found true rest,
safe within your love I dwell;
you shelter me from harm,
protect me in the storm,
in the shadow of your wings, my peace.

# 22

# Make a joyful noise to the Lord!

O come, let us sing to the Lord;
let us make a joyful noise to the rock of our salvation!
Let us come into his presence with thanksgiving;
let us make a joyful noise to him with songs of praise!
For the Lord is a great God,
and a great King above all gods.

*Psalm 95:1-3*

What a contrast there is in these verses with the encouragement to be quiet before God, to wait in the silence, expecting to find God in the 'still, small voice' that Elijah experienced in the mountains (1 Kings 19:12). In Psalm 95 the summoning call is to gather with others of like mind and heart with songs, shouts, praise, laughter, joy and exuberance, holding nothing back. For God deserves our heartfelt praise and worship, imperfect and inadequate though it may be. God is worthy: he is our Rock, Redeemer, Creator and Lord. The people are encouraged to submit with obedient hearts and acknowledge him as Lord of all.

Your church's tradition may tend to be somewhat more restrained than the corporate worship advocated by the Psalmist, and such extroversion may fill you with trepidation and fear! What about in the privacy of your own home? There are times when I am alone with God and quiet contemplative prayer simply isn't the answer. Reserved and very British as I am, a true introvert, my natural tendency towards meditation is sometimes abandoned in favour of a louder approach, although my friends and family might find it hard to believe! It fits the bill when my heart is bursting with praise for God – for who he is, for answered prayer, for an occasion when I know beyond doubt that his hand is on my life and that he cares about whatever concerns me – the big and small things alike.

So, abandon your inhibitions – if I can do it, so can you. Choose a moment when everyone else is out and your neighbours won't be disturbed and sing along at the top of your voice with your favourite praise and worship music. Maybe dance too – no one is watching! Experience for yourself how liberating and exhilarating such worship can be. Remember how King David 'danced before the Lord with all his might' in front of the Ark of the Covenant (2 Samuel 6:14), incurring the disgust of his wife, Michal, when she saw him 'leaping and dancing before the Lord' (verse 16)? If it was good enough for King David . . . Release your worship to God, then, as the Psalmist writes in verse 6, calm it down, and submit to your Lord and Saviour in awe and wonder:

O come, let us worship and bow down,
let us kneel before the Lord, our Maker!

*Psalm 95:6*

O worship the Lord in the beauty of holiness,
bow down before him, his glory proclaim;
with gold of obedience and incense of lowliness,
kneel and adore him, the Lord is his name.

*J. S. B. Monsell*

# 23

# Give thanks

Make a joyful noise to the Lord, all the earth.
Worship the Lord with gladness;
come into his presence with singing.
Know that the Lord is God.
It is he that made us, and we are his;
we are his people, and the sheep of his pasture.
Enter his gates with thanksgiving,
and his courts with praise.
Give thanks to him, bless his name.
For the Lord is good;
his steadfast love endures for ever,
and his faithfulness to all generations.

*Psalm 100:1-5*

In my Bible, this short psalm is headed 'a psalm for giving thanks, a call to praise the Lord', and I make no apology for including all five verses. The Psalmist tells us that we should worship God with joy and gratitude. He deserves all our praise and worship, for the Lord is King, a living and active God, our Creator who shepherds us with care, protection and guidance. The Lord is good, his love and faithfulness are everlasting, his grace and promises are trustworthy and true. Our thanksgiving should be spontaneous and heartfelt, for who God is, what he has done for us in Christ and for all he continues to do for us and in us.

There may be a tendency to confuse the call to give thanks with reasons to be cheerful. You might think that in today's world, there aren't many reasons to be cheerful. Watching the news bulletins for a few days may leave you feeling quite pessimistic and wondering when there will be anything good to report. It's easy to adopt a negative mindset and give way to complaining and grumbling, even if it's chiefly about the weather (if you're British!).

Try counting your blessings and begin each day with praise and thanksgiving to God on your lips, even before you climb out of bed. Be positive and with a thankful heart, remember his love and his goodness. I promise you, it's not simply trying to be optimistic, regardless of circumstances. Start a list of things you can be thankful for, both small and big blessings. Keep adding to your list day by day and be amazed how richly you are blessed by God.

My God, how wonderful you are,
your majesty how bright!
How beautiful your mercy seat,
in depths of burning light!

*Frederick William Faber, altered Horrobin/Leavers*

This is my story, this is my song,
praising my Saviour all the day long.

*Fanny J. Crosby*

# 24

# The greatness of God

Bless the Lord, O my soul.
O Lord my God, you are very great.
You are clothed with honour and majesty,
wrapped in light as with a garment.

*Psalm 104:1, 2*

The Psalmist uses creation to express the glorious might and majesty of God. We worship an awesome, all-powerful Creator who is invisible to our eyes, but his nature and glory are revealed in and through his creation. King David reflects on the greatness of God, as recorded at the start of Psalm 8:

O Lord, our Sovereign,
how majestic is your name in all the earth! . . .
When I look at your heavens, the work of your fingers,
the moon and the stars that you have established;
what are human beings that you are mindful of them,
mortals that you care for them?

*Psalm 8:1, 3*

David could well have been remembering his early life as a shepherd, out on the hills at night, in quiet and solitude, gazing up at the starlit sky and overcome by the beauty of God's world. In the light of God's greatness, he wonders why God even notices human beings. Yet we are the most valued part of his creation. As Jesus tells us, so intimate and complete is God's love for us, that even the hairs on our head are all numbered (Matthew 10:30).

Reflect on the majesty of God as shown in creation. You might want to go outside and enjoy the wonder of the night sky or another aspect of nature. You may have an image that is special to you – an actual picture, or you may carry the memory of a time that has particularly spoken to you of the greatness of God: a stunning sunset over a tranquil sea, perhaps, or the vivid colours of a rainbow.

If it helps, jot down any words that come to you about God's greatness and use them in praise and worship during your prayer times. It's so easy to look down or around and become discouraged. Look to God and be encouraged: your heavenly Father, Creator of all, loves you with an infinite love!

The Psalms repeatedly praise and thank God for who he is and for what he has done for us. Join with the Psalmist, as he responds in worship to the greatness of our God:

I will sing to the Lord as long as I live;
I will sing praise to my God while I have being.

*Psalm 104:33*

God is love: let heaven adore him;
God is love: let earth rejoice;
let creation sing before him,
and exalt him with one voice.
He who laid the earth's foundation,
he who spread the heavens above,
he who breathes through all creation,
he is love, eternal love.

*Timothy Rees*

# 25

# All God's love

Praise the Lord!
O give thanks to the Lord, for he is good;
for his steadfast love endures for ever.

*Psalm 106:1*

Other, very similar expressions of praise and thanksgiving for God's love are found in several of the Psalms. In our ever-changing world, God's love proves constant, faithful, never-failing and gives us security.

Some years ago, I was studying the Creeds as part of a distance-learning theology course and becoming more and more bogged down in the complicated ideas of the early theologians. A book on the Apostles' Creed by William Barclay was on the required reading list and I approached it with dread, expecting more difficult theology. Instead, I came across a chapter on the love of God the Father: the intimate love and fellowship he offers each of us. Barclay wrote about the love of God being tailor-made for each of us, intricate and personal, and how all God's love is given to each one of us. Barclay quoted from St Augustine, who said, 'God loves each one of us, as if there was only one of us to love.'*

Wonderful words. God gives us *all* his love, not simply a little bit. It's not like a huge cake that's divided up into slices, a small piece for you, or a few crumbs here and there. We are offered the *whole* cake – all God's love. This was one of those light bulb moments for me that stopped me in my tracks, a 'wow' moment, when a deeper understanding of God's love made the journey from my head to my heart.

All of God's love goes out to *you*. How safe and secure do you feel in God's love? Are you confident and assured of God's never-failing, unconditional love, acceptance and approval? God loved you even before you were born, before you had the opportunity to do anything, whether good or bad. He delights in you as part of his marvellous creation and loves you 'just as you are'. Nothing can change the way God loves you and nothing can separate you from this love (Romans 8:38, 39).

Think about the supreme gift of God's love in sending his only Son, Jesus, to die on the cross. A favourite image to look at may be helpful, or you might have a small wooden holding cross. Rest in God's presence and allow yourself to be loved by God. Even if you were the only person who needed Christ's sacrifice, he would still have gone to the cross to bring you salvation and eternal life. Contemplate this statement for a while. What is your response to this kind of love? I wish you the same as Saint Paul prayed for the Christians at Ephesus – that you may know the full extent of God's love for you and be filled to overflowing with all the fullness of God (Ephesians 3:14-19).

Oh the deep, deep love of Jesus!
Vast, unmeasured, boundless, free;
rolling as a mighty ocean
in its fullness over me.
Underneath me, all around me,
is the current of thy love;
leading onward, leading homeward,
to my glorious rest above.

*Samuel Trevor Francis*

* *The Apostles' Creed*, William Barclay, 1998, Westminster John Knox Press, Louisville, Kentucky, USA, page 32.

# 26

# My God

You are my God, and I will give thanks to you;
you are my God, I will extol you.

*Psalm 118:28*


Our creator God is so great – all-knowing, everywhere present and all-powerful, perfect in every way. Yet, as the Psalmist knows with all his heart and mind, he is *my* God. We can have a personal relationship with this wonderful God – how awesome is that! The words of the Psalmist are echoed by Thomas, who was privileged to encounter the risen Jesus in bodily form. Thomas believed and declared: 'My Lord and my God' (John 20:28). He was able to see, touch and hear Jesus; by the power of the Holy Spirit, Jesus is real and present with us today.

In his letter to the Philippians, Paul wrote of the 'surpassing value of knowing Jesus Christ my Lord'. Indeed, Paul regards everything else, his standing, past successes and achievements, as 'rubbish' by comparison (Philippians 3:8, 9). He's talking about more than knowing facts; his is a knowledge based on his experience of Jesus as his Lord and God.

Our relationship with God is more important than anything else. When everything else fades away, he is our hope and security, our solid rock and cornerstone. We are on a life-long journey into the heart and fullness of God's love.

Take some time to reflect on your own personal relationship with God. Can you honestly say, along with Thomas, 'My Lord and my God'? Or are you going through the motions, perhaps preoccupied with being busy for God and have lost sight of where he should be in your life – first and foremost, above all else? Are you busy fulfilling other people's expectations of you and feel swamped, having lost sight of your purpose and goals? Are you moving closer to the person God created you to be or is the real 'you' being side-lined somewhere along the way? Do you need to make any changes?

Take my love; my Lord I pour
at thy feet its treasure store:
take myself, and I will be
ever, only, all for thee.

*Francis Ridley Havergal*

# 27

# God's help

I lift up my eyes to the hills –
from where will my help come?
My help comes from the Lord,
who made heaven and earth.

*Psalm 121:1, 2*

This psalm is one of a series of fifteen 'Songs of Ascent', as sung by groups of pilgrims on their annual journey to Jerusalem, for one of the three major festivals. The hills in question were those around Jerusalem, one of which was Mount Zion. As the pilgrims began their climb, they may have felt daunted by the journey ahead, but they looked beyond the hills to the One who made them. Imagine standing at the foot of a steep hill or a mountain where you can't see the summit. A certain perspective is needed – the journey begins one step at a time.

In times of trouble, there is a tendency to cast our eyes downwards, preoccupied and swamped, focusing on the problem, instead of lifting our eyes up to God, the One who is the source of our help. If we lose sight of him, we can start to panic and flounder.

During life, we will all face situations that are impossible to handle without looking to God for help. Matthew 14:25-33 tells of Jesus walking on the water towards his disciples who were in a boat that was being buffeted by the waves. When Peter saw Jesus, he wanted to walk to him on the water, which was clearly impossible without divine assistance. Jesus told Peter to come to him and, initially fired up with enthusiasm and with his eyes on Jesus, Peter didn't doubt that he could defy gravity. However, when Peter focused on the wind instead, his fears overwhelmed him and he began to sink, crying out to Jesus in panic and desperation. Jesus reached out his hand and caught Peter, saying, 'You of little faith, why did you doubt?' (verse 31). They climbed into the boat together and the wind immediately died down – it had lost its power over Peter.

You find yourself on a hard journey, perhaps into unfamiliar territory. Who do you turn to for help along the way? Is God your first or last resort? What about those times when God seems distant or absent? In difficult times are you able to trust God's promises, even if you haven't much conviction of their truth? Writing a journal can prove to be a good source of encouragement to keep going on the journey of faith. Looking back at times of previous difficulties and seeing how God helped you through, can give you a better perspective on your present problems, and encourage you to keep going and not give up.

Heavenly Father, you are the one true God,
the Creator of everything,
all-powerful and my never-failing help.

You are my place of refuge
and a very present help in times of trouble,
protecting and guiding,
only ever a breath away.
Not a single sparrow falls to the ground
without you knowing.
I am more valuable to you than many sparrows
and I rejoice at the depth of your love for me.
I can put my trust in you,
knowing that you will never let me down
or stop caring about me.
Your promises are true and trustworthy
and I can depend on you.

# 28

# Whose work?

Unless the Lord builds the house,
those who build it labour in vain.
Unless the Lord guards the city,
the guards keep watch in vain.
It is in vain that you rise up early
and go late to rest,
eating the bread of anxious toil;
for he gives sleep to his beloved.

*Psalm 127:1, 2*

Psalm 127 is the only one of the 'Songs of Ascent' to be attributed to Solomon. Work can take up a great deal of our energy and attention; in order to be meaningful, our life's work must have God as its foundation. Without God's blessing on what we do, our achievements will be futile. We need to pray about our work, commit it to the Lord, thank him for his provision, and keep work in its proper place.

We hear a great deal about people who overwork: 'workaholics'. Characteristics are working too hard, not resting enough, pursuing a career to the detriment of family and friends and other areas of life, and looking to work as the principle way of finding security and fulfilment. Work becomes all-consuming and perspective is lost. The work-life balance is out of kilter, rest and refreshment neglected, with too much work becoming counter-productive.

It's crucial to maintain reasonable work levels. The other day I heard someone on the radio admit, 'I haven't done anything for fun for a long time', which struck me as profoundly sad. As Christians, there can be a tendency to focus on 'doing' – keeping busy (too busy?) in God's service. If we find ourselves without sufficient rest and spiritual refreshment, over-busy with meetings and 'good works' and neglecting our well-being, there's something very wrong. We can't substitute Christian service for a social life and God certainly doesn't want burnt-out followers. He wants us to care for and value ourselves.

Our well-being is sustained by taking enough time to slow down, relax, rest, have enough restorative sleep, eat a balanced diet and exercise regularly. The key to being fruitful lies not in frantic efforts but in abiding in God (John 15:1-11). Unless we spend enough time 'being' and listening for God's way forward, our 'doing' will become aimless and directionless, like a dog chasing its own tail. We are not defined by our work, by what we do, but by who we are in Christ.

A sign of not trusting God enough to provide for our needs, is that we take over control of our work and God is squeezed out. Do you think that your work-life balance is healthy? Is God excluded from certain areas of your working life? Do you feel God is blessing your work, or is it simply *your* work? How do you regard the Sabbath, the day of the week given by God for us to rest and recover, a time for reflection and worship? His commandment to keep the Sabbath is for our benefit and well-being.

O Sabbath rest by Galilee!
O calm of hills above,
where Jesus knelt to share with thee
the silence of eternity,
interpreted by love.

Drop thy still dews of quietness,
till all our strivings cease;
take from our souls the strain and stress,
and let our ordered lives confess
the beauty of thy peace.

*John Greenleaf Whittier*

# 29

# Contentment in God's presence

I have calmed and quieted my soul,
like a weaned child with its mother.

*Psalm 131:2*

Psalm 131 is another in the series of 'Songs of Ascent', sung by the pilgrims on their annual journey to Jerusalem, as they looked forward to entering the Temple to worship and enjoy God's presence. David paints a heart-warming picture of harmony and peace. He likens himself to a small child, resting in contented dependence with its mother. A quiet trust in God is the basis for his contentment. There is no restlessness or striving, no dissatisfaction. Instead, the Psalmist is at peace with God's leading in his life, knowing that this is how he will find his security and rest. David's love for his Lord is not conditional on what God does or doesn't do for him. David loves God for who he is: the Lord of his life and future.

Even (or, perhaps, especially) if your life is currently hectic and too busy, try to make it a priority to be still with God for a while and reflect on the sentiment of this psalm. If your prayer life has been reduced to a few snatched prayers 'on the hoof' as you chase through the day, easily distracted by a busy timetable, then learn to enjoy being with your Father without rushing away. Put aside your shopping list of prayer requests, rest in God's presence and be loved by him, set free to enjoy him for who he is, not for what he can do for you. God's desire is that we let him love us. Come to him in child-like trust, allow him to release you from any striving or restlessness and let him bless you with contentment. Surely such closeness to God is a treasure to be prized?

Your heavenly Father says to you:
Be still at heart, my child,
and let your striving cease,
in quietness and trust find rest;
like the petals on a flower
let my plans for you unfold,
entrust to me your hopes and dreams.

# 30

# Perfectly known and loved by God

O Lord, you have searched me and known me.
You know when I sit down and when I rise up;
  you discern my thoughts from far away.
You search out my path and my lying down,
  and are acquainted with all my ways.
Even before a word is on my tongue,
O Lord, you know it completely.

*Psalm 139:1-4*


In this well-loved psalm, we see a marvellous picture of our relationship with our heavenly Father. God is all-knowing, everywhere present and all-powerful; his knowledge and understanding of us is perfect. All our thoughts, words and actions are open before him, yet he still accepts and loves us unconditionally. Most wonderful of all, is that this perfect God, our Creator and Redeemer, allows us to know him.

It's possible to put up defences to stop other people from getting too close, or we may wear a protective 'mask' to hide behind, for fear that too much of our true self may be laid bare before other people. Alternatively, we may be running away from, ignoring or hiding from difficult emotions, such as fear and anger, covering them up, denying them and pretending that all is well.

With God there can be no pretence or hiding, our whole life is open to him and we are invited to be absolutely honest in his presence, holding nothing back. We may adopt the less than honest brave face with other people and be able to fool them (I'm fine, really . . .) but it's impossible to hide from God how we are feeling.

We come into God's presence exactly as we are. Any denial on our part will only hinder a closer walk with him. God is watching over us in love, not like a menacing Big Brother figure or an old-fashioned schoolmaster, waiting to punish us if we should step out of line. We have nothing to fear, for we are loved, cherished and precious to God and he is interested in every detail of our lives – body, mind and emotions. King David understood this and learnt to express every emotion before God, including blame and anger.

Sit quietly before God, holding nothing back. Visualise your life as a house. Are some rooms shut or locked to keep God out? What would it take to open those doors and let God in? Are you willing to do so? Tell God how you feel right now, share with him all that's on your heart: past regrets, present problems, future hopes and fears, feelings of sadness, loss or loneliness; in short, tell him where it hurts. If it's difficult to express in words how you feel, you could try using different colours and shapes to illustrate your emotions and feelings instead. No artistic skill is involved and no one else will see your drawing, unless you want them to.

Allow God's love to enfold you – it's a life-affirming love that can make you whole. Respond by expressing your love for him and be thankful.

Your heavenly Father says to you:
I have loved you with an everlasting love,
guarded you, the apple of my eye;
drawn you with cords of loving-kindness,
I have loved you with an everlasting love.